THE SPLOOGE FACTORY

The Splooge Factory

Christina Springer

Frayed Edge Press
Philadelphia, PA
2018

Copyright 2018 Christina Springer

Published by Frayed Edge Press in 2018

Frayed Edge Press
PO Box 13465
Philadelphia, PA 19101

http://frayededgepress.com

Cover image by Lita D'Vargas.

Publishers Cataloging-in-Publication Data

Names: Springer, Christina, 1964-
Title: The splooge factory / Christina Springer.
Description: Philadelphia, PA : Frayed Edge Press, 2018.
Identifiers: LCCN 2018939685 | ISBN 9781642510041 (pbk.) | ISBN
    9781642510058 (ebook)
Subjects: LCSH: Prostitutes -- Social conditions -- Poetry. | Sex workers
    -- Social conditions -- Poetry. | Sex-oriented businesses – Poetry. | BISAC:
    POETRY / American / African American | POETRY / Women Authors .
Classification: LCC PS3619.P753 S6 2018| DDC 811--dc22
LC record available at https://lccn.loc.gov/2018939685

For Michelle,
who opened the door
and invited me inside.
Rest now.
1964 - 2002

TABLE OF CONTENTS

Introduction

Michelle stood six feet tall. "Angular" best described her face and body, the exception being the Adam's apple in her throat. She wore her uncurlable, dark brown hair shoulder-length and straight forward. Her personality was like that also.

She had a knack for anything mechanical, but most loved building and programing computers. Like me, she saw the emerging internet as space, a vast and infinite territory. We viewed its possibilities differently, though. I saw potential for crazy innovations and new artistic genres. She saw potential for crazy innovations to support the oldest source of revenue generation known to women, the sale of sex-related services. She fascinated me. Everything about her was improper, defiant, contradictory, and raw.

Also like me, Michelle wasn't bound to a normal work environment. I was free because racism is expensive and I had proved it to a corporation during a well-negotiated exit strategy. She had found a way to do what she loved on the edges of society. In addition to being a "she-male" dominatrix, she managed several adult service establishments. Her dream was to make these services available online. It was 1998, the time when the internet was just opening up to the wider public.

She and my now husband would spend hours poking at machines and talking about code while I sat nearby playing with the use of html. I was trying to develop a method for publishing poems online which could deliver the collection in a non-linear, user-driven manner. They would help me solve technical problems. I would offer dinner or snacks. It was cozy until her pager would go off. She'd jump up, run out, and take the call. When she came back, I was always full of questions.

One night when they seemed to be having a work breakthrough, she had to leave. She returned quickly, so I asked her what had happened.

She said, "The call was for humiliation. I got to the house. He opened the door. I cracked my riding crop on the doorframe; looked him up and down and said, 'Take off all of your clothes.' He did. Then I laughed and said, 'You are not even worthy' and walked away."

"Noooo!" I giggled.

"Sometimes it works." She shrugged and went back to working on whatever it was that she and my husband had been doing.

Michelle seemed equally fascinated with my creative work. Having lived the majority of my adult life as a somewhat cloistered lesbian, my work was decidedly bisexual. (My husband was the first man I had been in a relationship with in over fifteen years.) At the time, I was writing and performing a lot of erotic work. Michelle was my best test audience. She loved my voice. She loved my cadence. She loved the way my body moved when I performd. She loved that I was sex-positive and non-judgmental. So, when her receptionist quit and she was short-handed, she asked me to fill in at what I began calling The Splooge Factory.

At first, answering the phones at The Splooge Factory seemed like a continuous exploration of sex, eroticism, and politics. For me the logical extension of "the personal is political," would be that all things related to being a person, including sex, become political. This all changed when I met my husband. I had a lot of catching up to do. I had a lot to learn.

My investigations of the erotic had been entirely lesbian and feminist. As a college student, I had eagerly read the dialogue between women during the sex wars of the 80s when Andrea Dworkin, Tee Corinne, Honey Lee Cottrell, and Susie Bright published frequently. Pat Califia's seminal work "Coming to Power" was the source of many discussions in the Womyn's Center at my college. Lesbian separatism had helped advance a body of sex-positive literature, performance, and films about sex and sexuality which centered on women. Womyn-identified erotica and sex play had another layer of intellectual rigor or political intention built into it.

During the short time I was at The Splooge Factory, I saw a huge difference. When I listen to White friends, of a certain age, discuss racism, what I usually hear is that the only information they received is that racism is wrong and makes you a bad person. As I began to listen to the desires of the clients, I began to understand that an honest, rigorous examination of racism and sexism had never occurred. Those of us who grew up during what I call the Failed Post Racial Experiment (1954 to 2016) had not been given critical information necessary to unravel internalized bias, prejudice, and stereotypes. These attitudes were instead forced underground.

People with means have the power to act out their fantasies. The ongoing progress towards a better, more inclusive world has consistently stripped White men of the normalization of and ability to act on their mental health issues related to how they cope with inferiority and/or need to be punished for their evil deeds.

The women whose stories are told in these pages are so much more than props in a male fantasy. They are full, complete, autonomous human beings. These women go to college. These women program computers. These women make art. These women are political activists. These women are daughters, aunties, spouses, mothers, friends. I cannot remember my preconceived notion about who a sex worker was before I met Michelle. I do know it was politicized, abstract, and feminist.

This book could have been a footnoted and indexed scholarly examination of all of these historic and contemporary issues. That is not what I do. Regardless, of all the elevated language and political theory I could attach to The Splooge Factory, what remains is the fact that Michelle opened a door. I walked through it. I am a poet. I tell stories. These are some of them. I'm opening the door to a very specific moment in time. Walk through with me.

SPLOOGE

Blessed   star path.
Progenitor   expedition.
Ancestor   pool.

Holy
milk.   Liquid
generations.   Tumescent
turbulence.   Ball bearing oil.

Hot
lead.   Putrescent
drop.   Explosive
utterance.   Wad.

Spunk.
Whore's   milk.
Dick   drink.
Snake   venom.

Baby
paste.   Goo.
Climax.   Mecotero.
Ejaculate.   Cum.

Joy
butter.   Cream O'
Baby.   Vitamins.
Fruit juice.   Protein shake.

Jizz.
Gism.   Love juice.
Pearl drop.   Organ
music.   Soul sauce.

Jazz.
Oyster.   Royal
jelly.   Mahu-pol .
Infant spit. Load.

Seed.

CANDY MAKES LESS OF AN INITIAL INVESTMENT THAN MARY KAY

All I need to do is strum
vocal cords. Create movie stud

pictures, thrust
eager sex tones

paint a bordello red fantasy.
Stage a quickening

heart breath.

I want you to come
spend money.

I need you plunging
desperate through the door.

I crave your huge
disposable income.

All day, watch the girls,
paint, lotion, exercise themselves

beautiful. All women would be -

200 dollars per week cures
ugly feet, uneven nails,

muscle tone. They earn
two grand. Cash profit.

On the phone, I flip
Ms. Magazine's pages;

push femininity falsehoods.
The older the man, the stronger

the urge to play pretend.
Brutality harsher the more

successful. I exploit
politically incorrect

yearnings. Knit
sexual satisfaction

from the unconscious
yarn of prejudice

using child's play
pretend games.

No sex. No genital touching.
Wages guaranteed

by silence and a work ethic
unique. America's daughters

join Clorox clean hands.
Snicker. When the men leave,

sing the praises of isms,
tax freedom,

power cheated.

LUNCH TIME
HE ASKS WHO IS WORKING

Asia
almond nugget,
rumored   to know
tea ceremonies.   5' 4

Ebony
gourmet hot cocoa
spiked with a shot
of spicy ghetto. 5'7

Salsa,
sizzling fajita.
Don't bite too quick,
she burns. 5'6

Vanessa,
clotted cream
with scones! Touch of saffron
hair.   5'8

Pamsie,
Irish potato
firm white flesh in a slick tan
skin.   5'5

Our specials today are:
Wrestling for $175 per half hour.
She-male dominant offered at $200 per half hour.
Two for one English –
ethnics not included.

Made to order are:
Breasts from 34 to 40 DD,
additional light or dark Black girls,
blonde Asian, big strapping Swede,
actual Arab Muslim – titties and pussy
not included in regular price.

May I take your order?

ORDERING DOUBLE DUTCH

Two black.
One mulatta-looking,
substitute Hispanic
if you're out of light-skinned

real Black girls.
I want them fresh,
authentic with ripe
butts. Only colorful

garnishes please.
Candy colored barrettes,
terry cloth hot pants, spaghetti
straps - the one shouldered

shirts I see everywhere
will do in a pinch.
But, I tip extra
if they know Down

In The Valley. Good.
Black girls will turn.
Mulatta jumps.
I want a good sweaty lather.

When I enter the room,
the two attack her.
Rip off clothing.
Bind her

in jump rope. Slap
her breasts, stomach and face
until I wrestle them
both to the ground.

I free her.
She beats them
until I cum
in their hair. Of course,

I'll pay the 50% deposit.
American Express or MasterCard.

FLY PAPER LINGERIE CANDY'S PERFORMANCE REVIEW, DAY ONE

Laid
scent

trails to girls.
Hung fly

paper. Paved

a sweet
glue street.

Dangled
a seductive

disembodied
voice between two

consenting phones.
Purred possibility.

Good afternoon,
my name is
                    ummm

Candy.
His name is

Herbert.
He needs me to expose

how I look. Like,
I'm just the voice.

EBONY – ACCOUNTS RECEIVABLE 1

The accountant shivers. I make him
bury his penis in a champagne

cooler. Shrink it blue.
Balls tense like a woman

alone at night clutching
pockets of safety.

Soon I will force
him into tight

women's clothes.
Shoes pinch him

smaller than I make him
teeter wiggle to disco.

Call him whore. Shove
a dildo down his throat.

Deny him more.
He wants to feel,

like a woman
revenge pays well.

ASIA WITH JACK

Ruffled panties crushed
against the concrete floor.

He pumps
lollipop

out. In.
Woman lips

grip Blow
Pop. Inside

innocence pushes. My irises –
gash memories – open

wide. Legs triangle
glittering jack rocks.

Sixies, I squeal.
Catching

balls in both hands.

FLY PAPER LINGERIE
CANDY'S PERFORMANCE REVIEW,
DAY NINE

The mystery is too much.
Herbert tangles my fly paper

into his webs. Wraps
me in questions.

Jams the phone lines.
Almost lost three bookings.

He has to own my image.
Panty size will do.

BEHIND HIS BACK,
CANDY CALLS HIM SAMBO

The first time he called, he wanted
to know if we accept Black clients.

Of course. We are an equal
opportunity splooge factory.

Do we have a blonde
to dominate him?

Redhead, blonde, blue,
black, brunette.

whatever. I smack
gum in his ear.

When he shuffles in
I appraise him. As if

being a sister gives me the right
to criticize his fantasies.

That's the problem with Black
women, always using

men's minds like trampolines.

That's why he comes here
to see white women.

They don't judge him.
The next time he wants

the blonde to call him nigger.
Okay, but, racism costs extra.

Vanessa must say nigger like she means it.
After seven weekly visits, he wants

only her. But, this time she must piss on him
as she screams nigger, riding crops his back.

At this point, I give him a web-address
for the KKK. It won't cost $200. He'll save

some money. Maybe get off.

EBONY PRETENDS NOT TO UNDERSTAND SAMBO (EVEN THOUGH SHE LIVES WITH THE PLANTER'S WIFE)

Civil War Reenactment,
circa 2002, she binds.
Wrists to antique
canopy bed. Turns up oil

lamp. Folds muslin skirt
to leave no tell tale
wrinkles or marks. Pins
petticoats to bloomers,

carefully pushes too deep.
Adorns. Bejewels me
in my blood. Drops
the ass flap; caresses

quivering flesh;
smacks hard. Laughs.
She yanks my laces.
Taffeta stretches tighter.

Whalebone forces
my brown shell upright;
She does not care
to break spine or skin.

Leaves me breathless
enough to barely stay
conscious. On the wall,

octoroon daguerreotypes
recall marrow deep
perversion. Eyes accuse,

You let
her tie you up?
You let
her beat you?

Yes, Mistress,
I whisper. She whips
me until I crack.   Peak.
Fold into a golden meringue

she eats slowly every time
we play the peculiar game.

FLY PAPER LINGERIE
CANDY'S PERFORMANCE REVIEW,
DAY TWELVE

Herbert calls everyday.

Look, I am not
being paid to stroke
your hairy feelers

I tell Herbert's short
breath. He offers
gifts if I reveal

what kind of cups
shape my shirt.
I hang up.

CANDY LEARNS EBONY IS A LESBIAN FOR NONE OF THESE REASONS

Water Melanin boys
hopelessly riddle.
Water Melanin boys
sour and shrivel
once plucked from the sweet
sturdy bush.

Leon - the only
appropriate
crush. His air
guitar platform

guaranteed him
the presidency of my love.
Sweet Home Alabama
was just another courtship

sound track stripping
away a dirtier brown than I could
remedy. My yellow yearning
for movie. Dinner. Date. Prom

illusion of first romance reminded
him of his inferiority. Even pink
Fair Isle sweaters
with lime green corduroys

could not discolor the fact
that we were both lost
puzzle pieces forcing
ourselves onto a Monopoly board.

Flat Black & White
school catalogue
pictures diversifying
private school hallways.

Water Melanin boys
hopelessly riddle.
Water Melanin boys
sour and shrivel
once tucked into dark
wooden crates.

Esby preached. Black
women need to tighten up
their borders from womb invasion
by The Man. Argues I
am a scared fertile trust
holding us together like spirituals
set the heart on safety.

Espy farms white women
like Chilean's produce summer
out of season. Silicon puffed
lips polished Delicious
Apple red. I bloom
with only a hint of airborne
moisture. His arms

around my shoulder confide
hot house flowers are too delicate
to survive the wind whipped
rocky Tundra of his soul.

His Black women press down
roots wherever he plants
them. That's why we have
to be patrolled. Nothing but raw
liquid assets. A net

profit of pure
strain. Resistant

to adversity. A field of hybrids
wilts under his hot air. Granules
of hope kick the wind like a mount.

Water Melanin boys.
hopelessly riddle.
Water Melanin boys
sour and shrivel
once plunked from the thick
sturdy bush.

Am I sexy? And Ahmed says:
My voice in his ears
is like anal penetration -
that intimate degrading

vulnerable beauteous
sacrificing gift fuck.
I titillate and tease
with intellect. When asked

Am I sexy? Ahmed said:
My thoughts slide in and out
of his soul. My strength
is twice as large as a mustard

seed. I am the kind of woman
that holds him in soft
pleasing hands on dark
desperate nights when flimsy
disposable flippant pussy can't be found.
When asked Am I sexy?

Ahmed said: I am deeper
than the kind of moment

a person wishes would last
forever. My back unbending
can hold any revolutionary's
future empire. I am both
dowry and wife.

Yes, Ahmed, but,
Am I sexy?

Water Melanin boys
hopelessly riddle.
Water Melanin boys
sour and shrivel
once tucked into dark
wooden crates.

CANDY BONDS WITH EBONY

Fetish or obligation. We exist
in plastic implants

under the skin. Invisible
to the naked eye. Costumed.

Compassionate whore. Savage wife. Too
big teeth or gasping tunnel

maw wet with rush hour traffic.
Subsisting on a posture of ingratiating

petulance. Cajoling visibility.
Never daring.   Knees held together

by men who have transformed our entire bodies
into the Black Power fists of youth.

Quick! Easy answers!
Do you love me? Quick!

Am I sexy? Just Answer!
Quick! Go the days I toss my humanity

to chase moments when
my body is loved in

deed and just
as much as my mind

Even monkey infants prefer
starvation in a soft embrace.

CANDY AND EBONY PURSE THEIR LIPS AS VANESSA TALKS ABOUT HER NEW BOYFRIEND

Dark,
meaty

man.
Gold

Benz,
matching

chains.
Personal

trainer
with extra

income.
I only date

Black men. Always
give it to me

up the ass.
Rough. So

I won't get
pregnant,

it makes me feel
better about myself.

SALSA ON CATECHISM
& IDEAL MEN

At seven, a Bride
Of Christ. Pretty

white lace
dress and veil.

Holy pure.
Pious, I knelt

mouth open
for the priest.

On my tongue,
he put Jesus.

It is wrong to bite,
so I sucked. Jesus

stuck to the roof
of my mouth.

Urgent tongue
flickers on his body.

He dissolved. Eating
before mass – taboo.

10:30 communion –
relief. Spiritual

hunger happens
because girls don't

suck noble, beautiful men.
The priest said so in CCD.

FLY PAPER LINGERIE
CANDY'S PERFORMANCE REVIEW,
DAY TWENTY-FOUR

He has seen
me, mark the girls
calendars. Redden
boxes with pseudonyms.

Con business suits.
Reassure each he is
the first, the favorite,
the real friend.

Eyes shutter.
Hips shift
in the easy chairs.
They hope

their girl really is
just painting her nails.
An envelope slides
through the mail

slot for Candy.

PAMSIE KISSES HER BOYFRIEND

Poke. Rub. Moan. No.
No mouth to mouth contact.
My touch indents

skin. Strangers
create meaning
from nothing.

Anonymous love.
Unreal. Two frank lips
Thrill. A life

with people that have names.

AT HOME,
EBONY PREFERS FISTING

Near death
or dream.
A door. Tunnel
widens. One finger

beckons in front
of cervix like angels
singing, *Stay.*
Stay! Hips sigh.
Parted. Deep

dusk breaths.
Two
fingers spread.
Knead.
Thrust need.
Sweat like resting
dough. Spine
rising.

Three, thrust. The first
orgasm – oven hot
swimming heat
haze. Legs spill
over shoulders.
Rising. Four,
oiled fingers

sizzle. Back
brown loaf arched.
Now. Five curl.
Clench. Break
like bread promises.

Relax to rhythmic
tender punching
passion. Vulnerability
at arm's length.

WHY SALSA NICKNAMED
HER NEW BEAU COACHWHIP

Downcast eyes. Sudden
flush, prickly

sweat bead, tongue
dashes to moisten,

lips. The energy between
waiting and touching.

In svaha, held
my chin. Heart

pound floundered,
forgets beating then,

continues. I dare
to live without rain.

Taut bare against sun
unrelenting. Pressed

mouths. Tasted
multiple lifetimes

flowering
in saliva.

My cellular memory
awakens like Ocotillo.

FLY PAPER LINGERIE
CANDY'S PERFORMANCE REVIEW, DAY THIRTY

Lingerie arrives daily
addressed to my perfect

fit. Herbert
calls. Always

one half hour
later. Begs me

to describe myself
between pants. Muffled

breaths
heavy. He wants

something new,
extra. Offers

to let me run
his credit card if

I tell him. *Everything*
but me is for sale.

PAMSIE WITH BILL

No single hint or clue.
Immaculately tailored.
Upright navy blue
banker solid.
I know his children
from his wallet. And tender

smiles. See him toss
tickle. Round
and round the island
kitchen. Two blondes.
A boy and a girl
in matching L.L. Bean

laughing. Every afternoon
I see his wife.
We can afford to shop
in the same places.
Pinch faced. Prim
she has earned her tight ass

and bears the sweaty weight
of beauty like a trophy.
Talbot's scarf knotted
just so. The way I do it
around his wrists and ankles
after pleasantries and cash,

but before the whip
makes him sob Mercy.
His daughter's name.

EBONY ATTENDS
BAND PRACTICE

At braid's end,
ribbons flutter.

White shirt tucked
tight. Uniform pleats

rise. Fan whirring
between my feet,

reveals crisp
clean cotton panties.

Lips snap gum bubbles.
Arms, breasts squeeze

the accordion
vigorously

open and closed
in time to his hand

conducting. Ear
splitting racket guided

by his dripping baton.

ASIA WITH PEDAR

Cupped reverent
gentle in his thick

hands. My foot
held as a holy

object. Stroked
like Buddha's belly.

Massaged. Decorated.
Worshipped like daughters

pray for tenderness.

SALSA WITH BUDDY

He can
crawl

now. I clap.
Squeal, *Look at*

da clever pretty baby
pookie boo so smart!

He gurgles,
Maaaa Ma.

Hands above his head
so I can steady wobbly

legs. He thumps down
on the mat. We play

paddy cake. Piggy his toes.
Tickle him. Check his diaper.

He yawns. Coos
when I give him a rattle,

so I can warm
his bottle.

Plaintive, urgent
wails, as I test

milk on my wrist.
Rub nipple on his mouth.

Coax him to suckle
Stroke his head. Soft

eyes trust wide gaze into mine.
Beard shadow, bristly

against my naked tender
breast. Remember lullabies

I once sang for minimum wage.

CHARLIE COMPLIMENTS EBONY

Sugar nigger lips,
pretty pouting

dick suckers.
Your women

were made
for pole greasing.

Pillows begging
for somebody to fluff

plump them.
But, curve

me a Jet beauty
smile. Honey,

blow me
a kiss,

before I churn
fat out of those buttery

Negress kiss biscuits.
Smear you with my super

special creamy
beauty lotion.

PAMSIE & THE MOTHER FUCKER

I hate his calm
smile, direct
eye contact, rain

drop on his index
finger. Lube glistens
before he jabs

my belly button.
Pumps.
Pulls his dry

cock, that little
wet hole watches
my fingered

navel. He circles.
Pokes. Rims.
Strokes that invisible

pulsing umbilical
ghost of cord.
Peeling

off my skin.
Forcing
a smile as he violates

my mother
line. Mommy
hollow.

Mama
button.
Coming between us.

CANDY EXPLAINS WHY
SHE ONLY ANSWERS PHONES

I couldn't
get laid

on prom night,
Red Joe couldn't

fuck me with fertility
goddess nipples.

Quarter sized
milk jets.

Oil slicks
tainting

heaving oceans.
My breasts

drowned
his sailor sized

erection.
Motherhood

siren song
scored with sepia

whole notes stained
his clean staff.

I do not inspire.

EBONY TELLS AN OLD WIVE'S TALE

Black women become
chemists not doctors.
Anything

wrong down there,
demanded Listerine.
Hiccups

marking strange
hours, sullen
withdrawal, smell

of testosterone's lingering
thump. The Listerine

douche bag. Cheap
no nonsense salvation.
Anything

unusual down there -
yeast scratch,
wiggle walk, boys

stuck in eyes, late
night coed
dancing in public

no room for the Holy
Ghost between you,
drunk naked
on rooftops - liquid

dry ice on labia.
Amber absolution
cotton swabbing
sin back

to hell. Sobbing. Mama
should have been a doctor.

SALSA EXPLAINS WHY SHE PREFERS DOMINATION TO NUDE MASSAGE

People assume I lie. I didn't learn
to masturbate until I was 22.
Somewhere back before free hair
and damnation, I had to go
inside at twilight.
Maybe I was eight when I danced –

wiggled like a naked stripper lady
in my bedroom window for an audience
of neighborhood boys. Eddie told me
he'd give me candy.
Tomorrow. He'd let me see
the pretty ladies I was starting
to look like one more time.

The CCD book asks:
Do you know what to do
when a friend shows you
pornography?

The CCD book answers:
You say "get real!"
Walk quickly away. Do not look
back. Do not invite people to sin.

I am directly responsible –
Eddie's flesh will peel, crack,
pop in the devil's bonfire.
He is not Catholic. Lust
in the brain is equal to fleshy
lust. He can never confess.

Neat questions and answers.
Masturbation – is it a sin? Yes!
Can dressing provocatively cause boys
to make repeated trips to the confessional? Yes!

What can be done? Improper
execution of penance leads
to eternal hellfire.

One joke caused orgasm to transcend
from fact to mythology. Weeks
before the dirty dancing incident
I crossed myself - "The Father, The Son" -
giggled and coyly, vaguely
touched my pubic region.

Repeated slapping clued me
in to a secret no one ever told me
outright. But, no punishment taught me
bodies are nasty sinful devil evil.
Mama prepared my salvation well before
any innocent sultry shenanigans,

Every night in the bath tub she
scrubbed me sacred raw. On top
of the closed toilet; stepping into bone
dry white cotton panties; elastic stretched
wide for the pouring of powder.
Thick white clouds choking.

Before she slipped
my hands into ivory clean socks,
she dipped them in cayenne powder;
clicked two safety pins on each
sleeve to hold them to the pajamas.
The walk to bed Gethsemane solemn.

Prayers and more prayers
mumbled into tub sock hands.
I tumbled into bed.
Arms crucifixion style
safety- pinned to the mattress. I slept

without ever turning over or rising to dream.

PAMSIE'S NIGHTMARE 1

Splooge
rivers swell.
Undulate over underground cash.
Hope - Ophelia bloated -
calls me. Mouth dropping sperm cell maggots.

ASIA PREPARES FOR VACATION

Hand stitching
medieval clothing
to camp. Two weeks

where men use large
bamboo sticks
to bash each other
on mock battlefields. Women

cheer their heroes. Nurse.
Cook. Market gossip.
Imbibe chivalry. Dance
aggression. Bonfires.

We all wear armor -
wenches, ladies and warriors.
Corsets, chemises and leather
remember simpler
more honest, civilized behavior.

SALSA VACATIONS

Rugged
mesas

jutting
phallic

formations.
Battering

the sky's
mouth. Goddess

absent.
I exist –

intermittent
clouds

devouring
prick rocks,

burn off
or blow away.

Father Sun,
Brother Wind

own this
turgid Earth.

EBONY EXPOUNDS ON CULTURAL SHIFTS REGARDING PERCEPTIONS OF BEAUTY AND FEMALE BODY IMAGE AS DEMONSTRATED BY THE CASTING, BLOCKING & PIVOTAL PLOT DEVELOPMENTS FOR PORN ACTRESSES

1935

Lily lesbians
frolic, thump.

Clumsy. Joy
seeking.

Silly girls
piano each other.

Silent lips
chattering

ragtime
giggles.

They pout.
Act goofy,

genuine.
Squeeze

eyes tight.
Guide each other

into the frontier.
Fresh, fleshy

Bodies. Untried
moving pictures.

1950

He begins flaccid,
it takes a lot of time
for her to harden him.

His eyes lovingly
caress her heavy hips,
hairy pudenda, arms and calves.

He strokes her head.
Teases her nipples,
gently, like a real

husband would touch
his wife in a modest
hard working bedroom.

1975

White hippies,
psychedelic room.

Two women,
a man befuddled

by his extraordinary luck.
And now what? Should he

kiss the true blonde
(fluffly v shaped proof)

or stoke the brunette's breasts
(thick forested arm pit valleys)?

His face contorts with confusion
rather than pleasure.

Honest desire.
He wavers.

Looks at each woman.
Immobilized with concern

about pleasing
both. Peace. Love.

Tuning out. Being in
two grooves at once.

2001

Fake breasts,
Shaved mounds.

Two platinum service
a man in stark raving color

as he stares off into space,
closes his eyes,

never touching the women
with anything but his cock.

CANDY EXPLAINS FUNK TAKES TIME
WHICH IS MONEY

He began
ordinary.

Cheap. Nude
massage. Seventy-five

dollars per half
hour. Over

the phone
line. I fish

for fetishes.
Gut. His desire

was affordable.
Until feet crept

into his booking
requirement: broad

flat worker's feet,
unpainted

toes with jam -
a cultivated

delicacy.
Perfect

bodies have a
shorter shelf-life.

Stink on feet
must be tended

hot house roses
bred for smell.

PAMSIE'S NIGHTMARE 2

Death's
garter belt
twists around my gyrating pelvis.
Thrust, baby. Hump, darling.
Empty fishnets dance. No legs inside.

CANDY PSYCHOANALYZES THE BLONDE WAITRESS OR THINKS SHE CAN READ EVERYONE'S MIND

Spilled vanilla
milkshake
          Blonde cumsluts gangbanged
          by Black stud monsters;

frothing pant leg. Blue
eyes. She dabs

          Ebony buck
          punishes trashy blonde;

a linen napkin
near my man's

          King Dong humiliates
          tight teen pussy;

crotch. Milk
Transubstantiates.

          Cock commandos
          conquer virgins.

Cum recalled. The electric line
between dilating pupils.

          Web searches
          disarm the dream. Plug

the mind's empty sockets.
Quickly, they avert their gaze.

SALSA CELEBRATES CHRISTMAS

On Christmas eve, bad
boys gobble discipline

like sugar cookies crumple.
Ben pays to decorate.

Fresh pine. Shiny red orbs.
Handcuffed. Ball-gagged.

Ben hangs limp
sprigs above each door. I decide

mistletoe begs illicit
illegal behavior. Beat Ben

for doing as he was told.
Whip him to straighten

slack twinkling lights
into a tidy five pointed star.

The window weeps,
Christ is Born.

CANDY LAMENTS THE TIMING
OF GYNIE APPOINTMENTS & A NEW MAN

Six month's waiting
to see how well
my toys
work. Like a child

opened gift - my
glossy wrapping
paper labia
lays exposed

on the examination
table edge. Thighs
patterned green
purple. Yellowing

bruises. Miniscule
lacerations. The gynecologist's
lips wrinkle. Earnest
eyes above privacy

cloth. Her mouth
hesitates. She wants me
to report some brutality
I do not remember. Blood

engorges each vein,
turns my skin Georgia
clay. Explaining
freak snow –

a Virginia boy –
loving me down
to the rind – lips,
teeth, hands gobbling

a plump Ruby Red
plucked from a Christmas
morning stocking in a whip
cream house before gifts.

VANESSA'S TRICKS OF THE TRADE

I patrol
my skin.

Magnifying
glass

enlarges all
small holes:

mosquito bites,
scratches.

My clothes
are a fortress

guarding
against rocks,

paper,
scissors.

These things wait
for clumsiness.

Tiny generals
eager to fire

catapults into my mud
and hay walls.

The army will invade. I'm not ready to fight
or die. Too young. Disease is watching.
It knows. It hungers for hot days when I forget to wear socks.

I forget sometimes. I like to look pretty the way Marilyn,
Janis, Jim and Jimi loved drugs. I wore
sandals. A sleeveless shirt. I must have
 a subconscious death

wish. I wish
a splinter

could not kill me.
Careful. I am

a clean girl.
Scrubbing myself

with bleach soaked
wash clothes

after every splooge
I create. I can not die.

EBONY WISTFULLY REMEMBERS HER ONLY BLACK GIRLFRIEND

1.

Flee.
Hide.
Don't
touch me there Daddy.
No.
Please.
Don't.
    Understand I am sacred,
       Scared,
       scarred.
Running.
Naked
shackles
    rip open tender virgin.
Stop.
Help!
Flush
out the animal.
      human
      woman.
See
wet
fur
    glisten wholeness power.
Musky,
thick,
helpless
    fear. Fear me. I am holy.
       terror
       breaking
chains.
Claiming
ownership
    self. Metamorphosis. Shredding,

tearing
paper
chrysalis
      press into forest scents.
                leaves.
                Decomposing
mulch.
Dung.
Dew
      renewing. Water throwing off hounds.
Drink.
Learn.
Taste
      zipper songs rasping safety.
                Drums
                pound.
Running
tongue
women
love each other in some promised land.

2.
She is bust of Nefertiti. Proud clacking braids kissing, savoring
teasing my hurt to peace. Fingers poke probe tickle. Liquor
unravels gold lapis lazuli visions. Leads me. Lost. Urgent.
Haplessly in debt to salvation. Licking

flat amber belly.
I am in bed with the desert. Lost. Fallow fertility. Sharp
water and thorns.
Sudden blossoms of miracle. Figs sticking gums to teeth.
Oasis.

S.O.S. Mayday! Plummeting into her terrifying transcendental
taste. I can't even love my own 18 years.
Have pressed kink out of my hair. Thinned
genetics beyond recognition. See my ancestors turn away

at the sight of me. How can I suckle the lips of history,
hear her smell story, drink my own reflection, rub Polaris?

3.

Zipper songs ripping
safety
open.

Running
tongue
women
love each other in some promised land.
Pound
drums.
Wade in

water.
Throw
hounds
out
of musky twilight

liquid celebrations.
Scarred,
scared,

sacred. Touch me there
lover -
in some promised

time - break
holy
terror.

I return
the call.

SALSA WHISPERS HER FIRST TIME

I am taking
my clothes off. One
piece at a time. One
shoulder. One starfruit
slice scar. Cheap red
lace forgets the time women
went delicately blind
for vanity. Lust. Two
clavicle. See.
Hunched shoulders
make salt wells.
How lucky! If I kept them
bowed
all the time humble,
a coke spoon
would fit
there nicely. One
garter unclipped. Two breasts
bray. Another garter unlatched.
After the stocking rolls over the foot,
it looks like a monster's condom
Imagine
something that big. Three
garters. Four.
My face must look funny
upside down. Hair sweeping
the floor. He says, *Maybe the whole house
should be cleaned this way.* Expensive
parquet floors, the mported Spanish
tile predicts my naked
pregnant body burning
in the kitchen, only the face left
unscarred by grease. Keloid- texture
thong strap peels off
like a large flake of dead
white sun-scorched skin. Awkward

headband snags the hair like modest hands.
What is left? The trite rose
tattoo from sweet sixteen. No
one was supposed to see.

EBONY – ACCOUNTS RECEIVABLE 2

Black
screen whirs.
User:/ hash L user
/bin unknown:
Finger: Mazur, Charlie
trace route:
5681-0341
Beeps
white
text.
SSN: 5681-034-1659
        Mazur, Charlie, Married
        5760 Bartlett Street
Pittsburgh, PA. 15212
        (412) 421-9409
        Employer: PNC Bank
        Title: Loan Officer

Ebony hums
        Getting to know you.

Perls on a Unix
terminal. Using user

information. Unnecessary,
hashing out

small securities.
Knowing, owning, holding

stolen data is more empowering
than Black

mail. Whining.

PAMSIE TALKS ABOUT
GRADUATING FROM CMU

I'm moving
to Florida. I conquered
education's debt

using good,
old fashioned, corn fed
entrepreneurial

skill. My limbs
swell heavy.
I have bloomed

a vibrant
verdant bank
account. Sin

compounds
my annual
interest rate.

After play acting
three seasons
of perversion,

Gonna teach drama
to freckle- faced
honest

girls. Untouched
by cash crops. Sexy
young

women ignorant
of my cunt-tree's
mouthwatering yields.

SALSA MEETS HER BOYFRIEND'S MOTHER

Clasped hands,
a hit and run kiss
caught by her rolling eyes.

Our unconscious
caresses plague
her senses. She bristles

when his foot slides
over mine; holds me
close; darting

hand to reassure himself.
I am near. Gagging
back bile, her words

probe for cracks
between us. She lowers
lashes. Sheepish

smile imitates
the way I shine
on him. She knows

his leg hair stops mid thigh,
below the ink splotch
freckle and those tiny two

higher. Wistfully coos:
One day, I'm going
to get a man just like you.

Mothers should not
say such things to sons.

BUSTED – CANDY'S FATHER

Your mother is nothing
but, a power broking whore.
Surprised about pandering?

You never learned
the sale of human flesh
is wrong. Your mother

sanctioned that man's cock.
Your 14 year old
mouth took repeated

greasy corporate
communion
daily. Silver

neck spikes
kept him from kissing
you. I knew.

You kept your neck,
safe. Unspoiled. She had
a thing for my Boss,

baby. It wasn't about
you or my ability
to provide. Honestly.

Mother's sins are paid
by daughters. Father
love finds

attorneys after the fact.

CANDY LOOKS BACK

Eye feel
triggers some perverse
anonymous monogamy
with strange men.
Thinking.
I am so special -

that unusual
set of knockers
keeping pothole rhythms
on the bus
without my clothes -
in some guy's struggle
to keep his penis publicly flaccid.
A distinguished fantasy.

Moonlight brings
dreamy lists. How many
men eyeballed me?
Was it luxurious wet
sticky serendipity?
Romantic?
Ho-hum missionary?
Violently erotic?
Just violent?
Phone number left on the _____?

Usually just *How much money could I have
made?*

PHRYNE

Whores will not be
kept from the safety

of your comfort.
Before Alexander

salted, women
poured secrets.

Scorn filled
huddle. High

tide eyes diminished
my shores. Good

women, begrudged
me their extra seed

and clean water
drawn in daylight

hours. Alexander pierced
the city's tender

skin. All life
holes salted,

ravaged. I rose.
Spit in his face.

No one knew
I hoarded

my harvests
for your protection.

NOTES

p. 1 - Putrescent Drop: The Talmud refers to semen in this way.

p. 5 - English: A slang word for being paddled.

pp. 25, 42 - CCD: Confraternity of Christian Doctrine or Catechism is the religious instruction given to Catholic children who attend secular schools.

p. 30 - Svaha: Origins for this word are found in Native American, African and Indian cultures. It means the sound between thunder and lightning.

p. 30 - Ocotillo (*Fouquieria splendens*) is a plant native to the American Southwest and northern Mexico. Another common name for it is Coachwhip. It is one of the oddest and most conspicuous desert flowers. During drought, it sheds its leaves to conserve moisture. Within 48 hours of a rain, it sprouts leaves and produces clusters of one-inch tubular red flowers.

p. 61 - Zipper songs: A type of song in which a word is easily "zipped out" and replaced by another, while attributed to Woodie Guthrie, this form predates him. Zipper songs were a form of code used by enslaved African-descended people. Words to well-known songs were modified or new verses were added to send covert tailored messages. Not to be confused with Zip Coon songs.

p. 64 - Perl: a programming language used mostly for internet applications.

p. 64 - Unix: a computer operating system capable of securely storing large amounts of data. Unix is also primary computer programming environment.

p. 69 - Phryne: After Alexander the Great destroyed the fortifications around Thebes, Phryne, a famous prostitute, offered to rebuild the city walls at her own expense on the condition that a plaque be erected which read, "Destroyed by Alexander and Reconstructed by Phyrne the Prostitute."

About the Author

Christina Springer is an Alt.Black artist who uses text, performance, video and other visual expressions to communicate what the space between molecules in the air wish for you to know. Cave Canem helped shape the multiple voices she advances with text. Poems have appeared in: "Gathering Ground: A Cave Canem Reader," "Saints Of Hysteria," "The Complete Idiot's Guide To Slam Poetry CD," *Obsidian, Fledgling Rag, Eyedrum Periodically, Red Headed Stepchild, The Mom Egg, The Comstock Review, Torch Literary Journal, The Drunken Boat, Janus Head,* and *Callaloo.* She taught creative writing at the University Of East London and City Lit College, London. Springer was the longest-reigning Pittsburgh Poetry Slam champion, from 1997 until 2001. She has also had five dance-theater scripts produced: "The Splooge Factory" produced by Composer's Collaborative, "Living Ancestry" and "Kikombe Cha Umpja: A Kwanzaa Myth" produced by Umoja African Arts Company, "Mary Magdalene & the Apostles" produced by The Acting Company, and "Life Rites" produced by City Theatre.